MAR 0 0 2015

W9-BLI-657

ADVENTURES ON THE AMERICAN FRONTIER

DISCOVERING THE WEST

THE EXPEDITION OF LEWIS AND CLARK

BY JOHN MICKLOS JR.

Consultant:
Jerry B. Garrett
Lewis and Clark Trail Heritage Foundation, Inc.
St. Louis, Missouri

CAPSTONE PRESS
a capstone imprint

Fact Finders Books are published by Capstone Press,
1710 Roe Crest Drive, North Mankato, Minnesota 56003
www.capstonepub.com

LIBRARY OF CONGRESS CATALOGING-IN-PUBLICATION DATA
Micklos, John.
  Discovering the West : the expedition of Lewis and Clark / by John Micklos, Jr.
      pages cm. —(Fact finders: Adventures on the American frontier)
  Summary: "Examines the Lewis and Clark Expedition by discussing the causes leading up
to it and the immediate and lasting effects it had on the nation as well as the people and
places involved"—Provided by publisher.
  Includes bibliographical references and index.
  ISBN 978-1-4914-0185-9 (library binding)
  ISBN 978-1-4914-0190-3 (paperback)
  ISBN 978-1-4914-0194-1 (ebook PDF)
1. Lewis and Clark Expedition (1804–1806)—Juvenile literature. 2. West (U.S.)—Discovery
and exploration—Juvenile literature. 3. West (U.S.)—Description and travel—Juvenile
literature. 4. Lewis, Meriwether, 1774–1809—Juvenile literature. 5. Clark, William, 1770–
1838—Juvenile literature. I. Title.
  F592.7.M48 2014
  978'.02—dc23   2014007814

EDITORIAL CREDITS
Jennifer Huston, editor; Sarah Bennett, designer; Wanda Winch, media researcher;
Tori Abraham, production specialist

PHOTO CREDITS
©James Ayers Studios, LLC; all rights reserved. Used with permission, www.jamesayers.
com, 24; The Bridgeman Art Library: Wood Ronsaville Harlin, Inc. USA/Matthew Frey,
17; Capstone, 7, 29; Courtesy Kathy Dickson, 11; CRIAimages: Jay Robert Nash Collection,
12; Getty Images Inc: Gamma-Rapho/Jean-Erick Pasquier, 8; Illustration by Keith A Lewis,
cover; James P. Rowan, 23 (bottom); Jim Carson, jimcarsonstudio.com, 5, 15, 16, 19, 20, 23
(top); Michael Haynes art, 13, 26; National Archives and Records Administration, 6 (b);
North Wind Picture Archives, 9; Shutterstock: 06photo, book page bkgrnd, brem stocker, 6
(t), homey design, leather design, Itana, sunburst design, ixer, 1 (banner), LongQuattro, wind
rose designs, Miloje, 18, Picsfive, grunge paper design, Spirit of America, 25; Washington
State Historical Society: artist Roger Cooke, 10, 21

PRIMARY SOURCE BIBLIOGRAPHY
Page 6—Kubly, Vincent F. *The Louisiana Capitol: Its Art and Architecture.* Gretna, La.: Pelican
        Pub. Co., 1977.
Pages 4, 14, 15, 18, 20, 26—"The Journals of the Lewis and Clark Expedition."
        http://lewisandclarkjournals.unl.edu/index.html

Printed in the United States of America in Stevens Point, Wisconsin.
032014   008092WZF14

TABLE OF CONTENTS

1

STRANDED IN THE WILDERNESS

A Vast Unknown Land

Heavy snow fell as the members of the Lewis and Clark expedition crossed the Bitterroot Mountains in mid-September 1805. After traveling for 16 months, the explorers were tired and hungry. Their supplies were running low, and there were few animals to hunt. They even had to kill some of their horses for food. But they pressed onward—up over the mountains and into history.

How did the members of Lewis and Clark's expedition find themselves in this difficult situation? What was their mission in this unexplored territory?

"I have been wet and as cold in every part as I ever was in my life, indeed I was at one time fearfull my feet would freeze in the thin mockersons which I wore ..."

—William Clark, excerpt from his journal entry dated September 16, 1805

Members of the Lewis and Clark expedition encountered heavy snow and icy rain when they crossed the Bitterroot Mountains in September 1805.

An Incredible Bargain

In 1803, the lands beyond the Mississippi River belonged to France, Spain, and Great Britain. Several American Indian tribes had also been calling those lands home.

What wonders might lie in that vast, unexplored land? President Thomas Jefferson wanted to learn about its plants and animals and befriend the American Indians living there. He also hoped to find a water route that led all the way to the Pacific Ocean. He knew exploring lands belonging to other countries might not be possible. But the Louisiana Purchase changed everything.

A Stunning Surprise

The Louisiana Purchase remains one of history's biggest bargains. For just $15 million (about $314 million today), the young United States doubled its size. That worked out to about 3 cents for 1 acre (0.4 hectare) of land.

This huge land deal stunned everyone, including President Jefferson. In early 1803, Jefferson asked **diplomats** James Monroe and Robert Livingston to buy the city of New Orleans from France. Napoleon Bonaparte, the ruler of France, surprised them with a much better deal. He offered to sell both New Orleans and 828,000 square miles (2,144,510 square kilometers) of land to the north and west. Monroe and Livingston didn't have time to get Jefferson's permission. A letter would take weeks to reach him across the ocean. So on April 30, 1803—without the president knowing—they signed papers to buy the land. Livingston said the deal would place the United States among the "first powers of the world." He was right.

Luckily, Jefferson was overjoyed when he learned about the Louisiana Purchase. Now his dream expedition could take place.

The Louisiana Purchase

Treaty Between the United States of America and the French Republic

diplomat—someone who deals with other nations to create or maintain good relationships

NEW LAND, NEW STATES

The Louisiana Purchase included land that would eventually become all or part of 15 states. These were Arkansas, Colorado, Iowa, Kansas, Louisiana, Minnesota, Missouri, Montana, Nebraska, New Mexico, North Dakota, Oklahoma, South Dakota, Texas, and Wyoming.

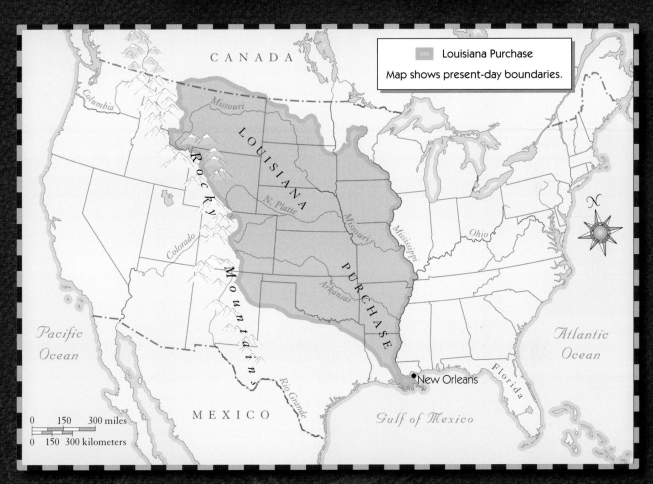

PREPARING FOR THE GREAT ADVENTURE

William Clark

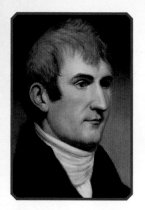
Meriwether Lewis

Jefferson asked his friend Meriwether Lewis to lead the expedition. Lewis invited his army buddy William Clark to be coleader. The 29-year-old Lewis was bold and daring, but he sometimes lost his temper. Clark, 33, remained calm in any situation. Despite their very different personalities, Lewis and Clark worked well together.

Planning for the Unknown

Lewis and Clark chose about 45 men to join their team, which became known as the **Corps** of Discovery. Some of the Corps members were soldiers. Others could hunt and navigate boats.

Lewis and Clark had a 55-foot-long flat-bottomed **keelboat** made that could carry tons of supplies. They also bought two large boats called **pirogues** in which the men rode.

Lewis and Clark had no idea what type of weather they might face or what animals they would find to hunt along the way. They packed tons of food, weapons, tools, and gifts for the American Indians.

Lewis studied with top scientists so he could write about new animals and plants discovered along the way. He also met with fur trappers and traders to learn all he could about what lay ahead. Clark trained the Corps members at Camp Dubois, about 20 miles (32 km) north of St. Louis, Missouri. The men learned to take orders and work as a team.

When spring finally arrived, the Corps members prepared to depart. These courageous men had no idea how long the journey might take or what dangers they might face. But they knew they were starting the adventure of a lifetime.

DEAR DIARY

Lewis, Clark, and a few other members of the Corps kept journals during the trip. They took notes about their progress, and Clark drew maps of the area the team was exploring. Lewis also wrote detailed descriptions of the plants and animals they discovered.

corps—a group of people acting together or doing the same thing
keelboat—a type of riverboat that is usually rowed, poled, or towed and that is used for freight
pirogue—a canoelike boat

CHAPTER 3

HEADING INTO THE VAST UNKNOWN

On May 14, 1804, the Corps of Discovery left Camp Dubois and began rowing up the Missouri River. Oars churned against the river's strong current, and gusty winds often rocked the boats. At times the men had to push or tow the heavy keelboat around sandbars. Some days they covered only a few miles. By day the men roasted under the hot sun and swatted mosquitoes. At night, they danced while crew member Pierre Cruzatte played the fiddle.

For food, Corps members caught fish and hunted wild game such as deer, elk, buffalo, and beaver. When game was scarce, they ate soup, cornmeal, dried apples, biscuits, berries, and roots. They often fought illnesses such as **malaria** and stomachaches. Despite the hardships, only one man died during the journey. Sergeant Charles Floyd's appendix burst in August 1804, and he died soon after.

Friends and Enemies

On August 2, 1804, the explorers finally met American Indians—members of the Otoe and Missouri tribes. Lewis and Clark tried to make friends with each of the tribes they encountered during their journey. They offered gifts such as beads, flags, and peace medals showing Jefferson as the "Great Father" in Washington, D.C. They explained that the land the Indians were living on was now owned by the United States. They said the tribes would benefit from trading with white men.

FINDING NEW SPECIES

As they moved further west, Corps members came across many plants and animals they had never seen before. They took samples of 178 new plants, including grand fir trees and the bigleaf maple tree.

On September 7, 1804, they found a huge village of prairie dogs. According to Clark's journal, they captured one alive by pouring "a great quantity of water in his hole." They sent the prairie dog back to President Jefferson the next year.

In all, they identified 122 new animals, including white-tailed jackrabbits, steelhead trout, coyotes, bighorn sheep, grizzly bears, and mountain lions.

malaria—a serious disease that people get from mosquito bites; malaria causes high fever, chills, and sometimes death

YORK

William Clark brought his slave, York, with him on the journey. Strong and brave, York did everything the other crew members did. When the crew voted on where to camp for the winter in 1805, York got to vote too.

Most American Indian tribes had never seen anyone with black skin before. One chief even rubbed York's skin to see if the color would come off.

After the expedition, York asked Clark to set him free. Clark finally agreed—but not until 10 years later.

Settling in for the Winter

In late October, the Corps met the friendly Mandan and Hidatsa tribes in what is now North Dakota. Snow had already fallen, so the explorers built their winter camp near the tribes' villages. They called their camp Fort Mandan.

While there they met a fur trader named Toussaint Charbonneau. He offered to be an **interpreter**. Lewis and Clark hired him, but they believed his pregnant wife, Sacagawea, might be even more helpful.

Sacagawea grew up as a member of the Shoshone tribe. Lewis and Clark believed Sacagawea could help show other tribes that the explorers came in peace.

The Corps struggled through a brutal winter at Fort Mandan. Some men suffered **frostbite** as temperatures plunged as low as minus 45 degrees Fahrenheit (minus 43 degrees Celsius). They passed the time visiting, hunting, and dancing with their American Indian friends.

interpreter—a person who can tell others what is said in another language
frostbite—a condition that occurs when cold temperatures freeze skin

Corps members built Fort Mandan to survive the first winter of their trip.

After months of being snowed in, the Corps members were eager to get started again. Little did they know that their second year of travel would be even more challenging than the first.

CHAPTER 4

DANGERS AND TRIUMPHS

In early April 1805, several men took the keelboat back to St. Louis. They carried maps and reports of the expedition's progress. They also took plant samples and live animals, including the prairie dog they had captured the year before.

Meanwhile, the rest of the explorers moved westward in pirogues and smaller dugout canoes. Lewis knew they were entering a dangerous unknown land. Still, he called the moment of departure "among the most happy of [his] life."

Water, Water Everywhere

The Corps faced danger throughout their journey. On May 14, 1805, a sudden gust of wind nearly **capsized** a pirogue. Sacagawea bravely helped rescue valuable tools, books, and medical supplies.

In late May the Corps members could see the Rocky Mountains in the distance. Lewis viewed them as a milestone of their progress. But he worried about the "sufferings and hardships" ahead.

On June 13, Lewis spied the Greats Falls—one of a series of waterfalls in present-day north-central Montana. In his journal, he described them as "the grandest sight [he] ever beheld." The Corps found the falls much less grand when they had to **portage** their boats and supplies nearly 20 miles (32 km) around them. They built crude wagons to carry the boats. For nearly a month, they worked to get past the falls. Bears, rattlesnakes, and prickly plants that ripped through their clothes only added to their woes.

The Great Falls were an incredible sight, but it took the Corps almost a month to get around them.

capsize—to tip over in water
portage—to carry a boat or supplies over land from one stretch of water to another

Captain Lewis met members of the Shoshone tribe whose friendship proved to be very valuable to the Corps.

A Joyful Reunion

After finally getting past the Great Falls, the massive, snow-capped Rocky Mountains loomed ever closer. Winter comes early in the mountains, and the Corps had to get across before snow started falling. But they could not cross the Rockies in boats. They needed to find horses. Luckily, Sacagawea began recognizing landmarks from her youth.

Lewis took three men and went ahead of the rest of the group. On August 12, they crossed the **Continental Divide** near what is now the Montana-Idaho border. They hoped to find a great river running due west toward the Pacific Ocean. Instead, mountains stretched as far as their eyes could see.

Their luck improved the next day when they met some Shoshone, who led them to a large camp nearby. The Corps members spent several days with the Shoshone until Clark's group caught up with them on August 17. That day marked an amazing twist of fate. When Lewis and Clark met with Cameahwait, the Shoshone chief, they brought Sacagawea along to translate. When she saw Cameahwait, she realized he was her brother. They had been apart since childhood, so they were happy to see each other. The Corps traded weapons and ammunition for 29 horses and soon pushed onward. They left behind their canoes, hoping to use them again on their return trip.

Sacagawea and her brother, Cameahwait, shared an emotional reunion.

໑ **FUN FACT** ໑

West of the Continental Divide, rivers flow west, emptying into the Pacific Ocean. East of the divide, rivers flow east and drain into the Atlantic Ocean.

Continental Divide—an invisible line that splits North America into two parts

"The Most Terrible Mountains"

Upon entering the Bitterroot Mountains (part of the Rockies), travel became even more difficult. It only got worse as the Corps struggled through icy rain and heavy snow. When food ran out in mid-September, they had to eat some of their horses. Since turning back was just as dangerous as moving forward, they slowly pushed onward.

Finally on September 21, they straggled out of the Bitterroots into the land of the Nez Percé in present-day Idaho. The Nez Percé fed the strangers and helped them regain their strength. The Corps stayed with the tribe for a couple of weeks. While there, the Indians showed them a different way to make canoes.

"[We] have no meat of any kind. Set in to raining hard at dark so we lay down and slept, wet, hungry and cold."

—Joseph Whitehouse, excerpt from his journal dated September 3, 1805

The Corps trudged through deep snow as they crossed the Bitterroot Mountains.

In early October, the explorers resumed their journey. They took boats down the Clearwater, Snake, and Columbia Rivers. The canoes risked capsizing, so Chief Twisted Hair helped them navigate the dangerous rapids.

Now traveling with the current, the Corps members raced toward the Pacific Ocean. They still faced rapids and waterfalls, but they were getting closer to their destination.

On November 7, Corps members saw a large body of water ahead. "Great joy in camp," Clark wrote. "[W]e are in View of the Ocian." But he was wrong. They had merely reached the Columbia River **Estuary**. They were still some 20 miles (32 km) from the Pacific Ocean.

Bad weather stranded the Corps for several days in the Columbia River Estuary.

Finally, on November 15 they reached the Pacific Ocean in what is now Washington.

On November 24, Lewis and Clark called for a vote to decide where the Corps would spend the winter. Even York and Sacagawea got to vote—decades before either blacks or women were allowed to vote in elections. It was decided that they would build their winter quarters on the Columbia River near present-day Astoria, Oregon. They named the settlement Fort Clatsop after a nearby American Indian tribe.

Corps members celebrated when they finally reached the Pacific Ocean.

The Corps of Discovery suffered through another long, dreary winter. It rained nearly every day. The explorers passed the time by hunting and drying meat. They also made moccasins to protect their feet on the long journey home. By spring, everyone was eager to head home.

✒ FUN FACT ✑

William Clark estimated that they had traveled 4,162 miles (6,698 km) to reach the Pacific Ocean. Even without any scientific tools for measuring distance, he was only about 40 miles (64 km) off in his calculations.

estuary—the wide part of a river where it joins a sea

CHAPTER 5

RETURNING HEROES

On March 23, 1806, the Corps of Discovery began the long journey east. The trip home went much more quickly because they were traveling with the current for most of the way. They also found faster routes in some places.

The explorers also saved time because they now had friends among the American Indian tribes. They didn't have to spend time introducing themselves and explaining their mission. With the help of the Nez Percé, they crossed the Rocky Mountains on horseback in late June.

In early July after spending a few days in present-day Montana, Lewis and Clark decided to split up for a while. Lewis took one group due east to explore the Marias River. Clark took another group south to retrieve the canoes they'd left behind the previous year and build some new ones. Then they continued down the Yellowstone River.

Clark and his group explored the area along the Yellowstone River.

On July 25, near present-day Billings, Montana, Clark came across a giant sandstone formation. He named it Pompys Tower (now called Pompeys Pillar) after Sacagawea's young son, who was with him at the time. Clark carved his name into the soft stone.

William Clark's signature on Pompeys Pillar is still visible today.

The Corps members took a big risk by splitting up. Had they run into hostile American Indian tribes, their smaller groups could have easily been outnumbered. In fact, in late July Lewis' group killed two Blackfoot warriors who were trying to steal their guns and horses. Fearing revenge from other Blackfoot warriors, the explorers raced 120 miles (193 km) on horseback over the next 24 hours. Remarkably, this was the only bloodshed between the explorers and American Indians during the entire journey.

In late July 1806, Lewis' group encountered a fierce bunch of Blackfoot warriors.

Reunited

On August 12, Lewis and Clark's groups reunited in what is now North Dakota. Soon after, they reached the Mandan villages, where they stayed for several days.

When they left on August 17, the explorers said good-bye to Sacagawea. She and her family stayed behind with the Mandan. As a guide and interpreter, the brave young woman had been a valuable member of the team.

Traveling with the current and the wind, the Corps flew down the Missouri River. They covered as much as 80 miles (129 km) a day. Some stretches that took a week to travel going out took only a day or two coming back.

OUCH!

While out hunting on August 11, Corps member Pierre Cruzatte accidentally shot Lewis in the thigh. Lewis was dressed in **buckskin**, and Cruzatte mistook him for an elk. The injury wasn't life threatening, but for several days, Lewis had to lie facedown in his canoe because he couldn't sit. By early September, his wound had healed, and he was able to walk again.

✧ FUN FACT ✧

In the United States, there are more statues of Sacagawea than of any other woman.

buckskin—a strong, soft material made from the skin of a deer or sheep

25

Home at Last

On September 23, 1806, the Corps of Discovery arrived in St. Louis. It had been nearly two and a half years since they began their journey. Joyous townspeople greeted them as heroes. Most were amazed that the explorers were still alive.

"...[T]he people of the Town gathered on the bank and could hardly believe that it was us for they had heard and had believed that we were all dead and were forgotton."

—Sergeant John Ordway, excerpt from his journal entry dated September 21, 1806 (when the Corps arrived in St. Charles, Missouri, about 20 miles (32 km) from St. Louis)

Lewis' dog, Seaman, jumped off the boat as the Corps arrived back in St. Louis.

President Jefferson was delighted to hear that the Corps had returned safely. Congress gave each Corps member twice the wages he had been promised and 320 acres (129 hectares) of land. Jefferson rewarded Lewis and Clark with 1,600 acres (647 hectares) of land.

What Happened to the Heroes?

In 1807, Lewis became the governor of the Louisiana Territory. He died of a gunshot wound on his way to Washington, D.C., in 1809. He was only 35.

Clark was named head of Indian Affairs for the Territory of Louisiana in 1807. From 1813 to 1820, he served as governor of the Missouri Territory. He died in 1838.

Most experts believe Sacagawea died of disease in South Dakota in 1812. However, others believe she lived to old age and died on a **reservation** in Wyoming.

Her son, Pomp, grew up to become an American explorer, fur trapper, military scout, and gold miner during the California gold rush. He also briefly served as the mayor of an area in Southern California.

reservation—an area of land set aside by the U.S. government for American Indians

OPENING THE NEW FRONTIER

The Corps of Discovery covered roughly 8,000 miles (12,875 km) during its remarkable journey. The expedition set the stage for westward expansion. By the 1840s, thousands of people were moving out west.

But as settlers pushed further west, they squeezed the American Indians from their homelands. Meanwhile, the United States grew into a world power, partly through the riches gained from the western lands. The Louisiana Purchase proved to be one of the greatest bargains in history. And the Lewis and Clark expedition was one of history's greatest adventure stories.

TIMELINE

1803
The Louisiana Purchase doubles the size of the United States. Lewis asks Clark to join him as coleader of the expedition to explore the western lands.

November 11, 1804
Lewis and Clark meet Sacagawea, a young Shoshone woman who will prove valuable to the expedition.

November 7, 1805
The Corps think they have reached the Pacific Ocean, but it is actually the Columbia River Estuary.

1803

1804

1805

May 14, 1804
The Corps of Discovery departs up the Missouri River.

November 15, 1805
The Corps of Discovery reaches the Pacific Ocean.

THE ROUTES OF LEWIS AND CLARK

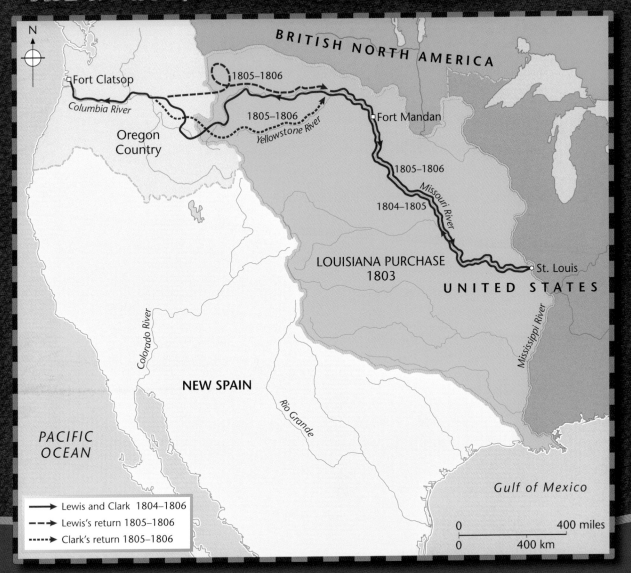

BRITISH NORTH AMERICA

Fort Clatsop

1805–1806

Columbia River

Oregon Country

1805–1806

Yellowstone River

Fort Mandan

1805–1806

Missouri River

1804–1805

LOUISIANA PURCHASE 1803

UNITED STATES

St. Louis

Mississippi River

NEW SPAIN

Colorado River

Rio Grande

PACIFIC OCEAN

Gulf of Mexico

→ Lewis and Clark 1804–1806
--▶ Lewis's return 1805–1806
····▶ Clark's return 1805–1806

0   400 miles
0   400 km

March 23, 1806
Lewis, Clark, and the Corps of Discovery head for home.

1806

1807

September 23, 1806
The Corps of Discovery returns to St. Louis where they are welcomed as heroes.

1807
Lewis is appointed governor of the Louisiana Territory. Clark becomes head of Indian Affairs for the Territory of Upper Louisiana.

GLOSSARY

buckskin (BUHK-skin)—a strong, soft material made from the skin of a deer or sheep

capsize (KAP-syz)—to tip over in water

Continental Divide (kahn-tuh-NEN-tuhl duh-VYD)—an invisible line that splits North America into two parts

corps (KOR)—a group of people acting together or doing the same thing

diplomat (DIP-luh-mat)—someone who deals with other nations to create or maintain good relationships

estuary (ESS-chu-er-ee)—the wide part of a river where it joins a sea

frostbite (FRAWST-bite)—a condition that occurs when cold temperatures freeze skin

interpreter (in-TUR-prit-uhr)—a person who can tell others what is said in another language

keelboat (KEEL-bote)—a type of riverboat that is usually rowed, poled, or towed and that is used for freight

malaria (muh-LAIR-ee-ah)—a serious disease that people get from mosquito bites; malaria causes high fever, chills, and sometimes death

pirogue (PEE-rohg)—a canoelike boat

portage (POOR-tij)—to carry a boat or supplies over land from one stretch of water to another

reservation (rez-er-VAY-shuhn)—an area of land set aside by the U.S. government for American Indians

READ MORE

Domnauer, Teresa. *The Lewis & Clark Expedition.* Cornerstones of Freedom. New York: Children's Press, 2012.

Gondosch, Linda. *Where Did Sacagawea Join the Corps of Discovery?: And Other Questions About the Lewis and Clark Expedition.* Six Questions of American History. Minneapolis: Lerner, 2011.

Sanford, William R. *Sacagawea: Courageous American Indian Guide.* Courageous Heroes of the American West. Berkeley Heights, N.J.: Enslow Publishers, 2013.

Schanzer, Rosalyn. *How We Crossed the West: The Adventures of Lewis and Clark.* Washington, D.C.: National Geographic Children's Books, 2012.

Stille, Darlene R. *The Journals of Lewis and Clark.* Documenting U.S. History. Chicago: Heinemann Library, 2013.

INTERNET SITES

FactHound offers a safe, fun way to find Internet sites related to this book. All of the sites on FactHound have been researched by our staff.

Here's all you do:

Visit *www.facthound.com*

Type in this code: 9781491401859

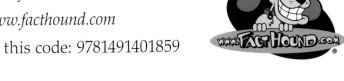

Super-cool stuff! Check out projects, games and lots more at **www.capstonekids.com**

CRITICAL THINKING USING THE COMMON CORE

1. How does the map on page 29 help you better understand the text and the explorers' progress? (Integration of Knowledge and Ideas)

2. How does the author support the claim that the Louisiana Purchase was a good investment for the United States? (Key Ideas and Details)

3. The author presents some of the information in this book in a chronological format, highlighting key dates from the expedition. Why do you think he chose this style, and how does it suit the presentation of the information? (Craft and Structure)

INDEX